RICHMOND PUBLIC LIBRARY, CA 94804-1659

3 1143 00594 4427

D0568172

Richmond Public Library

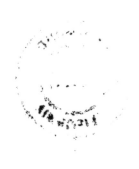

Unidentified Flying Objects and ExtraTerrestrial Life

Carole Marsh

Series Editor:
Arthur Upgren, Professor of Astronomy
Wesleyan University

RICHMOND
PUBLIC
LIBRARY
CALIFORNIA

Twenty-First Century Books

A Division of Henry Holt and Company
New York

Twenty-First Century Books
A division of Henry Holt and Company, Inc.
115 West 18th Street
New York, New York 10011

Henry Holt® and colophon are registered trademarks of Henry Holt and Company, Inc.
Publishers since 1866

©1996 by Blackbirch Graphics, Inc.
First Edition
5 4 3 2 1
All rights reserved.
No part of this book may be reproduced in any form without permission in writing from the publisher, except by a reviewer.

Published in Canada by Fitzhenry & Whiteside Ltd.
195 Allstate Parkway, Markham, Ontario L3R 4T8

Printed in the United States of America on acid free paper ∞.

Created and produced in association with Blackbirch Graphics, Inc.

Photo Credits

Cover (background) and page 4: ©NASA; cover (inset) and pp. 6, 13, 16, 34, 36, 43: ©Photofest; pp. 9, 26: ©Science Photo Library/Photo Researchers, Inc.; p. 11: ©David A. Hardy/Science Photo Library/Photo Researchers, Inc.; pp. 15, 20, 31, 39, 40, 41, 48, 51, 52: Photri Inc.; page 18: ©W. Hille/Leo de Wys, Inc.; p. 24: Photo Researchers, Inc.; p. 28: ©Julian Baum/Science Photo Library/Photo Researchers, Inc.; p. 54: ©Ken Biggs/Photo Researchers, Inc.; p. 57: ©David Parker/Science Photo Library/Photo Researchers, Inc.

Library of Congress Cataloging-in-Publication Data

Marsh, Carole.
    Unidentified flying objects and extraterrestrial life / Carole Marsh. — 1st ed.
       p.   cm. — (Secrets of space)
    Includes bibliographical references and index.
    Summary: Discusses efforts to find intelligent life on other planets and theories on this topic and describes UFO sightings and other phenomena that are given as evidence of extraterrestrial visitors among us.
    ISBN 0-8050-4472-8
    1. Life on other planets—Juvenile literature. 2. Unidentified flying objects—Juvenile literature. [1. Life on other planets. 2. Unidentified flying objects.] I. Title. II. Series.
QB54.M353   1996
001.9'42—dc20
                                      96-18571
                                          CIP
                                          AC

TABLE OF CONTENTS

INTRODUCTION

Humans have always been fascinated by space, but it has been only since the 1950s that technology has allowed us to actually travel beyond our Earth's atmosphere to explore the universe. What riches of knowledge this space exploration has brought us! All of the planets except Pluto have been mapped extensively, if not completely. Among the planets, only Pluto has not been visited by a space probe, and that will likely change soon. Men have walked on the Moon, and many of the satellites of Jupiter, Saturn, Uranus, and even Neptune have been investigated in detail.

We have learned the precise composition of the Sun and the atmospheres of the planets. We know more about comets, meteors, and asteroids than ever before. And many scientists now think there may be other forms of life in our galaxy and beyond.

In the *Secrets of Space* series, we journey through the wondrous world of space: our solar system, our galaxy, and our universe. It is a world seemingly without end, a world of endless fascination.

—Arthur Upgren
Professor of Astronomy
Wesleyan University

While exploring the question, "Are we really alone?" people have invented many kinds of alien life.

CHAPTER 1

ARE WE REALLY ALONE?

"Are we alone?" is a question that has always intrigued people. This question leads to many others: Are we the only humanlike life-form in the universe? Have extraterrestrials—beings from another planet—ever visited Earth? If not, are they on their way? If they *are* coming to Earth, what do they want? What do they look like? What will we say to them, and they to us?

These are indeed fascinating questions. They keep many people awake at night, wondering about our universe, wondering whether we are alone—or not!

Some men and women spend their lives doing more than simply asking themselves whether extraterrestrials exist. Exobiology is the search for and study of life outside of the Earth and its immediate atmosphere. Exobiology is sometimes also called astrobiology. A person who has decided to become an exobiologist, or astrobiologist, must study chemistry, physics, biology, space science, and much more to prepare for the search for extraterrestrial life. Carl Sagan, a famous professor of astronomy and the director of the Laboratory for Planetary Studies at Cornell University, in Ithaca, New York, believes it is probable that other planets in space sustain life. In fact, many scientists firmly believe that life, including complex life-forms, can indeed be found elsewhere in the universe.

They base their belief on the fact that Earth, the Sun, and our Milky Way galaxy are not unique in space. There are more than 100 *billion* stars in our galaxy. Even if only one star in a million has an Earthlike planet revolving around it, as our Sun does, there would be about a half million planets in our galaxy alone that could support life. And our galaxy is just one of 100 million galaxies that scientists believe may exist in our universe. So, these scientists say, there should be plenty of opportunity for life to form in other places in the universe—perhaps, in a countless number of places.

When scientists speak of discovering life elsewhere in the universe, they are referring to two kinds of life-forms. One is simple, single-cell life, or SCL. Algae and bacteria are examples of this type of life-form. The other is intelligent, technological life, or ITL. Humans are an example of this type.

So far, no evidence of SCL has been found in our solar system. Because we are limited by the vast distances of space and the slowness of even our most advanced space probes, we have been unable to look for SCL beyond our solar system.

However, we are able to search for intelligent life within and beyond our solar system. Using instruments called radio telescopes, scientists have been looking for evidence that life exists elsewhere in our universe.

Scientists believe that intelligent life beyond our planet would produce signals that could be detected by radio telescopes. These scientists, called radio astronomers, use the telescopes to search the skies, hoping to encounter these signals. By using this

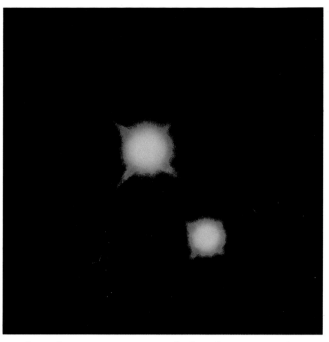

Radio telescopes can search the skies around Alpha Centauri A and B, in hopes of encountering intelligent life.

method to look for ITL, scientists are unlimited by the distance away from Earth they can search. For example, using current technology, it would take almost 40,000 years to travel from Earth to Alpha Centauri A and B, the nearest stars besides the Sun. But by using radio telescopes, scientists might be able to receive extraterrestrial signals from these stars today.

Scientific searches for extraterrestrial life are very different from people's sightings of an Unidentified Flying Object (UFO), or the supposed abductions of humans by alien beings. So far, no proof has ever been found that any UFO is a spacecraft sent to Earth by aliens. And there has been no evidence to prove that abductions by aliens have occurred. Scientific searches for alien life are carefully organized. They involve methodical searches seeking evidence that will prove without dispute that such life exists. And if they do find such evidence, our world will never be the same!

Even as you read this book, radio messages may be being sent toward Earth. So far, we have not detected any. But there may one day be a signal . . . if we are not alone.

The Strange Universe

Clearly, many people are convinced that extraterrestrial life exists. Some also believe that Earth has been visited by UFOs— unidentified flying objects that are often called "flying saucers."

A UFO is any object that moves through the sky, can be seen by the human eye or detected by radar, but that cannot immediately be identified. UFOs are often described as moving impossibly fast or as hovering in the sky, in a way that no earthly aircraft has yet achieved. They have been reported to be disk-, cigar-, or ball-shaped, quiet or noisy, flashing with multicolored lights, or shimmering with a silvery glow. Some are even said to emit a terrible odor.

Most unidentified flying objects turn out to be airplanes, weather balloons, clouds, meteors, the aurora borealis (northern lights), natural phenomena, or some other identifiable object. Some sightings, however, are never explained. But this only makes them unidentified—not necessarily flying saucers.

There is no proof that extraterrestrial life exists or that flying saucers soar through Earth's skies. However, our universe is mysterious enough that some people believe anything is possible.

Among the kinds of real or theoretical space phenomena that intrigue people are black holes. When a star dies, its core becomes so dense that it finally collapses. Its powerful gravitational pull causes the star to cave in on itself, resulting in a "black hole" that sucks in all the star's matter. Not even light can escape. Some scientists wonder whether black holes are the key to taking shortcuts through the universe to move from one point in space or time to another, faster than the speed of light. If so, they speculate, perhaps extraterrestrial spacecraft are already able to travel around the universe using black holes.

Other scientists believe that black holes may be gateways to an entirely different dimension of space called hyperspace. Supposedly, through this hyperspace, matter could travel around in

An artist's view of how black holes might be used as "tunnels" for traveling through dimensions of space.

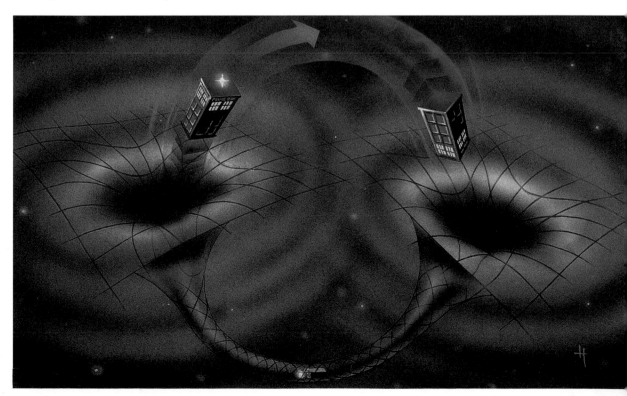

a different time dimension than the one that exists on Earth. For example, a spaceship could pass through this hyperspace as if it were a secret passage. Theoretically, the spaceship could end up in a part of space light-years away, much more quickly than would be possible in space as we know it.

Some scientists suggest that other worlds may exist that are not visible to us. If alien beings live on planets in this theoretical parallel world, they may use black holes like tunnels to travel into and out of our world.

Only continued research can bring about the new discoveries needed to prove or disprove such fascinating theories, including the existence of life in outer space.

Writing Through Time

It is hard to know what to believe when it comes to extraterrestrials and UFOs. No matter where or when, if people think they are seeing something as amazing as a UFO and its occupants, they are inclined to record the historic event in some way. According to numerous written accounts, people throughout history have spied strange flying objects. Thousands of years ago, the pharaoh Thutmose II reported smelly disks of fire and ice speeding silently through the skies over Egypt. His 3,400-year-old papyrus diary states that "fishes and winged creatures" fell out of these bright circles.

Two ancient epic poems, the *Mahabharata* and the *Ramayana*, were written in India at least 2,000 years ago. Both tell of disk-shaped flying machines called *vimanas*. In the Bible, the prophet Ezekiel noted that around 600 B.C. a strange, fiery

Movie "Stars": The First Aliens from Hollywood

Almost as soon as there were moving pictures, there were science-fiction movies. The first sci-fi movie was produced in 1902. It was called *Journey to the Moon*. By the 1950s, science-fiction movies filled the theaters. Images of rocket ships and their strange occupants were just as popular then as they are now.

Such movies as *The Man From Planet X*, *The Day the Earth Stood Still*, *Forbidden Planet*, and *It Came From Outer Space*, chilled spines and inspired imaginations to go wild. Movie aliens ranged from grotesque, terrifying invaders to kind and gentle creatures who had come to help save us from ourselves.

Some of these extraterrestrials were big, bug-eyed monsters, while others looked remarkably like humans—or suspiciously like the actors who played them.

These movie-star aliens got to Earth in a variety of ways. Some came in plant spores embedded in meteorites. Others rode in elaborate spaceships that look ridiculously old-fashioned today. While special effects were used, they were not the sophisticated, computer-generated wonders that we see in movies today.

But in all of the movies, the theme was basically the same: We are not alone. "*They*" are out there, and, "they" are coming. Get ready!

Early science-fiction movies, such as The Man From Planet X, *first sparked our imaginations with visual images of spacecraft and aliens.*

cloud in the sky lifted him up and carried him off to another world. Roman writers also told of fiery round shields and burning globes appearing in both the day and the night skies, some of them falling to Earth.

In A.D. 747, enormous fire-breathing dragons, followed by men in airships, were reported flying in the skies over China. In A.D. 900, three men and one woman reportedly stepped out of an airship in Lyon, France, and were mobbed by astounded onlookers. In 1666, Russians leaving a church saw an odd-looking fireball hovering in the sunny sky over their village of Robozero. And in August 1883, according to witnesses in Zacatecas, Mexico, more than 400 cigar- and disk-shaped objects moved across the Sun.

Art and Aliens

Another way in which people have recorded what they have seen is through art. Cave paintings in France and Spain depict objects that look like modern-day spacecraft. These drawings are more than 20,000 years old. One of the paintings shows a figure standing beside what looks like a spaceship. What *did* these cave people see or believe that made them draw early UFOs, complete with antennae and landing gear?

A woodcut by Hans Glaser, a famous German artist, shows the skies over Nuremberg, Germany, on the morning of April 14, 1561. In it, cylindrical objects appear to spit out black, red, and orange balls. Artwork by another artist features what looks like a sky battle over the town of Basel, Switzerland, on August 7, 1577.

The movie *Chariots of the Gods* questioned whether this figure, found on a temple in Central America, was in fact an ancient astronaut.

People have used whatever artistic means were available to record what they have witnessed. In West Africa, for example, sand paintings seem to depict alien beings and their spacecraft. A design carved on an ancient Mayan tomb lid looks like an astronaut flying a space capsule. A prehistoric pictograph in a cave in Italy shows a creature wearing what seems to be a space helmet. And ancient rock paintings in Peru feature people who also appear to be dressed for space travel.

Extraterrestrials in Contemporary Literature

Modern science fiction is filled with aliens and UFOs as varied as the most vivid imagination can invent. The popularity of such books and the movies they often inspire is ample evidence of our deep interest in extraterrestrials and their spacecraft.

"Little green men"—a popular term for extraterrestrials— is believed to have come from the science-fiction magazine *Amazing Stories* in the late 1940s. Harold Sherman was the author of stories such as "The Green Man" and "The Green Man Returns," about an alien who could read people's minds. Other UFO literature has included references to humanoid-type extraterrestrials that have green skin or wear green clothes.

Green has long been a popular color for fictional aliens, such as this extraterrestrial woman from an episode of the TV show *Star Trek*.

Noah's Space Ark

Why would aliens, supposedly far superior to humans in technological knowledge and skills, want to visit Earth? Some theories suggest that extraterrestrials are trying to escape from their own dead or dying planets.

Some ufologists—people who study UFOs—think that spacecraft from other worlds are arks that were launched into space when it was obvious the aliens' home planet would be destroyed. It has even been suggested that it would be wise for earthlings to build space arks in the event that we have to evacuate our planet in an emergency one day.

The themes of some science-fiction movies mirror this ark theory. In these films, extraterrestrials visit Earth not to attack us but to warn us to mend our ways so that our planet will not suffer a catastrophic end like theirs did.

When scientists talk about disasters to the environment such as nuclear winter and the greenhouse effect, the advice that earthlings build space arks seems more and more sensible. Perhaps space stations, if they are constructed, could fill this need for a refuge from our own folly, or from a fate that is beyond our control.

In 1968, Erich von Daniken published *Chariots of the Gods.* This bestselling book tells of visitors from other planets to Earth in ancient times. Most scientists, however, have expressed great doubt about the author's ideas. For example, von Daniken proposed that gold artifacts from the Incan culture represented otherworldly spacecraft and that long stretches of land in Peru may have been prepared as runways upon which alien ships could land.

Author Erich von Daniken proposed a theory that the statues on Easter Island may have been created by aliens.

Von Daniken also suggested that aliens trapped on Easter Island, off the coast of Chile in the Pacific Ocean, carved the strange and mysterious stone statues found there. These statues seem too large to have been created with the primitive tools that ancient humans had. What is more, the figures bear no resemblance to the island dwellers or their ancestors. Von Daniken proposed that the gigantic statues may have served as a call for help to fellow aliens searching from the skies for their stranded friends.

Von Daniken also wondered, as others have, how the ancient Egyptians built the Great Pyramid, which is made up of more than 2 million blocks of stone, each weighing thousands of pounds. It has been suggested that visitors from outer space provided the technology. Still, skeptics wonder why the aliens used stone instead of space materials.

Answers from Aliens?

As we have seen, the history of many civilizations includes references to visits by extraterrestrials to Earth in folklore and art. Further evidence may perhaps also be found in people's advanced knowledge of astronomy and other scientific matters. For example, the Dogon people of Mali, in West Africa, insist that their tribe was visited by inhabitants of the star Sirius. These alien beings supposedly taught the Dogon much about astronomy, knowledge that was unknown elsewhere on Earth until thousands of years later.

Could ancient peoples truly have learned about space from alien astronauts? Or did their knowledge come from contact with other earthlings? For example, did their information come from scientifically knowledgeable cultures such as those of the Egyptians and the Babylonians? Perhaps they gained their sophisticated knowledge from missionaries and explorers.

It is clear that people throughout the ages and from all parts of the world have observed many strange space-related phenomena. Again, however, it has never been proven that what they witnessed actually came from outer space. No matter how dramatic the apparent "evidence" of visits by aliens or how much fun it is to think about such things, only one thing will convince scientists that extraterrestrials and UFOs exist: undeniable proof. Nothing else will do.

The powerful, radio-radar antenna in Arecibo, Puerto Rico, is being used to listen for unique signals, possibly being sent by intelligent life.

CHAPTER 2

SEARCHING THE SKIES

One of the most outstanding events in the history of humankind would certainly be the day we make contact with a being from outer space. Will that day ever come? Many scientists are working to speed up and improve the search for such a being.

SETI: The Search for Extraterrestrial Intelligence

Project Ozma was the first serious search for life beyond Earth that used a radio telescope as its primary tool of investigation. In 1960, astronomer Frank Drake (considered to be the trailblazer of the SETI field) searched for extraterrestrial signals using a 85-foot (30-meter) telescope at the National Radio Astronomy Observatory in Green Bank, West Virginia. During a two-month period, Drake aimed the telescope at two stars

66 trillion miles (106 trillion kilometers) away. Although no extraordinary signals were detected, the project promoted the study of radio signals as a way to locate intelligent life.

In 1992, the National Aeronautics and Space Administration, or NASA, initiated a $100 million program to search for extra-terrestrial life. Its goal was to prove, beyond a shadow of a science-fiction doubt, that there is indeed life elsewhere in space.

NASA's primary tool in this endeavor was a 20-trillion-watt radio-radar antenna, the most powerful ever built. It is based in Arecibo, Puerto Rico. The Arecibo telescope system is a 1,000-foot- (305-meter-) wide bowl of perforated aluminum that nestles in a hole in the ground. Hundreds of tons of antennae are suspended above the bowl from cables. In turn, these cables are attached to a network of support towers anchored in the nearby hills.

Using the Arecibo telescope, along with a global network of radio telescopes, more than 100 astronomers, physicists, computer programmers, and technicians began to search. Super-computers were tuned in to millions of radio channels. The hope was that they could identify a signal that was unique because it had been originated by another life-form.

The difference between NASA's program, called High Resolution Microwave Survey (HRMS), and earlier investigations was HRMS's improved equipment and methods. Powerful computer programs were used to interpret intercepted signals. So sophisticated was the new equipment that more "listening" for extraterrestrial signals was done in three days than had been done in the previous three decades. The HRMS project, however, ended in 1993 due to lack of government funding.

As part of NASA's HRMS project, an all-sky survey was performed using a radio telescope. This type of survey looked for signals throughout the universe, and was performed at NASA's Goldstone Deep Space Network tracking station in the desert near Los Angeles, California. At the same time, other telescopes were used to search for signals from stars close to our galaxy. For example, in addition to the Arecibo telescope in Puerto Rico, the Parkes telescope, located 220 miles (354 kilometers) from Sydney, Australia, scanned radio waves in search of extraterrestrial life.

When the HRMS program ended in 1993, scientists at the SETI Institute in Mountain View, California, formed Project Phoenix to take its place. Scientists at observatories worldwide focused on more than 1,000 stars in a systematic sweep of the sky. No alien signals were received as a result of this search.

Scientists who have been determined to continue the search for alien life have often had to struggle to find funding and other support for their projects. The popular astronomer Carl Sagan cofounded the Planetary Society in 1982 to raise money and support for ongoing SETI projects. Steven Spielberg, the director of the movie *E.T. The Extra-Terrestrial*, donated $100,000 to help fund the Megachannel Extraterrestrial Assay (META). This search was conducted in 1985 from Harvard University's Oak Ridge Observatory in Massachusetts. In October 1995, the META project became the Billion Channel Extraterrestrial Assay (BETA).

Scientists believe that the key to a successful SETI program is the radio telescope. This instrument is similar to a television satellite dish. The radio telescope directs the radio waves that

Carl Sagan has done a great deal to popularize astronomy and has supported the search for life on other planets.

hit it toward a central collection point. There, the signal is directed to a receiver and processed.

Radio waves given off by stars are different from those used in communication. Star-generated radio waves are random and irregular. In contrast, communication radio signals appear as regular patterns on display monitors. Scientists believe that intelligent beings elsewhere in the universe might also communicate through regular radio frequencies. Thus, some scientists believe, it may be possible to intercept an interstellar alien message by searching for such signals among the star static.

The types of searches using radio telescopes vary. An all-sky search, as described, covers the universe. An example of a more tightly focused search would be a search of the Horsehead Nebula, which is the most prolific birthplace of stars that we know of. Such stars as Beta Pictoris, which is 56 light-years away and surrounded by space dust that may be

Jill Tarter, Leader in the Search for Extraterrestrials

Sometimes at school, you are asked to fill out forms that identify the occupations of your parents or guardians. If you were Shana Tarter, when it came time to pencil in Mom's job, you would write "Searches for extraterrestrials."

Jill Tarter was the lucky astronomer who got to pull the switch that began history's most ambitious search for life in outer space. She had worked long and hard to become the leader of the Arecibo, Puerto Rico-based HRMS project, launched by NASA at 3:00 P.M. on October 12, 1992.

As a child in Eastchester, New York, Jill Tarter was a fan of early science-fiction television shows, such as *Flash Gordon*. Tarter says that she grew up "comfortable" with the idea of alien life. When she was a college student, she sometimes walked on the beach at night with her father, looking up at the sky and discussing the life-forms that might live there.

In 1976, Tarter received a doctoral degree (an advanced degree from a university) in astronomy from the University of California at Berkeley. She then worked at the Ames Research Center in California studying stars. Her interest in extraterrestrial life led her to begin conducting research in this area. In 1988, Tarter was named project scientist, HRMS's top position at NASA.

Jill Tarter feels lucky to be in this field at this time. Today, the search for life beyond Earth is taken much more seriously than it was in the past, when researchers in SETI programs were often ridiculed and had difficulty finding funding and resources for their work.

What happens if Jill Tarter and her team members determine that a signal from outer space picked up by the radio telescope in Puerto Rico definitely is alien in origin? She explains that in this event, they would immediately make the information public. Such a message, she explains, would be directed not to her or to NASA only, but to all the people of our planet.

The Horsehead Nebula, in the constellation Orion, is a good location for a highly focused search for alien radio signals because it produces more stars than anywhere else known to us.

forming planets, are other likely sites for the detection of an extraterrestrial communication.

What would happen if an appropriate message were intercepted? Most likely, the operators of the experiment would be notified automatically by e-mail. The astronomer on duty would search the signal, reposition the telescope to catch any possible repeat of the signal, and alert scientists at other observatories so that as many people as possible could try to confirm the message. When all alternate possibilities were eliminated, there would be only one conclusion left: We are not alone!

In the early 1970s, people working on the "Big Ear" SETI project at Ohio State University had an experience that was exciting. A researcher on duty noticed an unusual signal, one so different from the others being received that he wrote "WOW" next to it on the computer printout. Unfortunately, neither this signal nor other similar signals were ever repeated. They are still considered unexplained mysteries. But these types of false alarms are what keeps patient searchers motivated for the long, hard task of discovering life in outer space.

What is the probability of a successful SETI program? No one knows for certain. However, we do know that if we do not search, our chance for success is zero.

Flying Saucers

In 1896, hundreds of Californians claimed to have seen a "great airship" in the skies over Oakland and Sacramento. Soon afterward, many sightings of a large, cigar-shaped object were reported. Some people said that the oblong object had wings. Others insisted that they heard the sound of a motor and saw a beam of light from the ship, and figures moving around inside. (It is interesting to note that it was not until 1900 that Germany launched its airship called the zeppelin. And Orville and Wilbur Wright did not get their flying machine up off the sands of Kitty Hawk, North Carolina, until 1903.)

Constable Kettle of Peterborough, England, reported hearing the sound of a buzzing motor overhead on the night of March 23, 1909. He saw a bright light in the sky and then a dark, oblong object that zoomed off into space.

Similar reports came from Europe for many years. In Norway, Sweden, and Finland, "ghost-fliers" were reported. These appeared to be airplanelike machines that flew low over snowy, foggy mountains like phantoms in the night. The ways in which the aircraft moved were considered impossible at the time.

In World War II, American pilots described small balls of colored lights that seemed to play tag with their fighters and bombers during both the day and the night. The soldiers called these mysterious objects "foo fighters," after a saying in a popular comic book that meant "crazy fire."

Even after the war, when, one might think, weary survivors would not have been surprised by anything flying overhead, there were thousands of reports of "ghost rockets." But no explanation of exactly what they were was ever provided.

What were people seeing? Some said that the American sightings were hoaxes. The British, the Germans, and the

Ball lightning (shown in this artist's view) might be the source of some UFO sightings. Although not proven to exist, there have been many reports of people seeing ball lightning, both indoors and out.

Danes all accused one another of concocting fake UFOs. And serious searches were made of Russian and German air bases to determine whether they were the origin of spy planes that might have been misinterpreted as UFOs.

Sightings Galore!

The year 1947 marked a flood of UFO sightings in the United States. Between June and July alone, 850 sightings were reported.

An event occurred on June 24, 1947, that marked the beginning of the modern era of UFO sightings. Airplane pilot Kenneth Arnold was on a routine flight when he spotted nine crescent-shaped, silver objects speeding over the Cascade Mountains in Washington. He said that they moved like "a saucer skipping over water." A newspaper reporter abbreviated his description to "flying saucer." People have been calling unidentified flying objects "flying saucers" ever since.

Despite many sightings, there were no explanations of what these aircraft were. One thing, however, seemed clear: They were not flying themselves.

Flights Over France

At least 100 witnesses spotted a UFO over a town in southwestern France on October 27, 1952. Its cigar shape was almost the same as that of a spacecraft that had been reported ten days earlier in a town a little more than 100 miles (161 kilometers) away.

In August 1954, a French businessman reported that he had an actual encounter with a UFO. He said that it had lasted almost

Project Blue Book

A pilot's report of a UFO over the state of Washington in 1947 set off an unprecedented flood of similar stories around the United States. By 1948, the U.S. military felt forced to respond to the American people's growing demand for an explanation. Thus, "Project Sign" was established to research UFO sightings and to determine, if possible, what the UFOs actually were. Researchers supposedly concluded that UFOs might represent visits by aliens in spacecraft. The project was then discontinued.

From 1948 to 1952, the project (now called Project Grudge) resumed investigating UFO sightings. In 1952, its name was changed to Blue Book. Investigative procedures included interviews with eyewitnesses of alleged UFOs and the analysis of photos of alleged UFOs. Most sightings were deemed to be hoaxes, hallucinations, or misidentifications. Only a few sightings could not be explained by conventional means. The project was discontinued in 1979.

Many people, however, believe that a group of people searching for extraterrestrial life resumed their work from an underground room called the Tank, located at the Pentagon in Washington, D.C. Supposedly, the group was formed in 1987 after an unidentified flying object was seen streaking across U.S. airspace. The air force monitored the strange object's flight, which reached a speed that no earthly craft was capable of attaining. The flight was officially labeled "unidentified," and no further explanation of its nature has ever been given.

It is difficult for the public to understand what was discovered during these various projects, since much of the information obtained remains secret. Although the media often report alleged cover-ups by the government of actual UFO activity, no one has ever proved that there is any truth to such charges.

an hour. The man had just pulled his car into the garage of his home near Paris when he glanced up and saw a large, glowing, cigar-shaped object hovering silently in the sky. As the man watched, the bottom of the craft opened. A disk fell out and then sped away. Soon a second, third, and fourth disk emerged from the base of the hovering ship. After a while, a fifth disk detached itself and swooped overhead. The man reported that he could very clearly see its circular form and red glow. The sighting was never explained.

Most sightings, however, *are* explained. Sometimes it takes a while for the truth to be told because the UFO is in fact a top-secret military aircraft. Stars, lights, and other natural phenomena mistaken for flying saucers are more quickly explained. And most hoaxes are eventually exposed. Still, around five percent of sightings remain truly "unidentified."

These clouds over Brazil could easily be mistaken for flying saucers.

Close Encounters

To see a UFO zipping across the sky is one thing. To see, meet, speak to, touch, or be abducted by an alien life-form is quite another. Such an event is called a "close encounter."

The accepted definition of a close encounter with a UFO is an encounter during which the object comes within 500 feet (153 meters) of the witness. A Close Encounter of the First Kind is the simplest and most common such sighting: The UFO is seen at close range but does not actually land. A Close Encounter of the Second Kind involves a spacecraft that affects Earth and/or its inhabitants. The effects may include flattened vegetation, scorched earth, panicked animals, stalled automobile engines, dimmed headlights, and radio interference.

Most dramatic is a Close Encounter of the Third Kind. For such an encounter to occur, witnesses must actually see the UFO's occupants. To date, the only reported Close Encounters of the Third Kind have involved just one or two witnesses. Almost all of the alleged incidents happened at night, and the aliens apparently did not try to communicate with the humans.

The Scoutmaster

One night in 1952, Scoutmaster Sonny Desvergers was driving three Boy Scouts home near West Palm Beach, Florida. He spotted a mysterious light, stopped the car, and set off to investigate. He told the boys to call for help if he did not return shortly.

When their scoutmaster did not return after a while, the nervous boys summoned the police, who appeared just as Desvergers staggered back to the car. He was almost in shock, with his face and arms burned and his cap singed. But he was able to explain that he had made his way to a clearing, walking toward the flashing light. Once there, he had almost passed out from intense heat and an odd smell. Above him was an enormous metallic disk. When he aimed his flashlight toward it, the disk spewed red light, and Desvergers fell to the ground unconscious.

An investigation showed that grass roots in the clearing had been charred by a heat source up to 300°F (149°C). Such heat, which would produce sparks and ozone, could have accounted for Desvergers's burns and the odor he experienced. Although the U.S. Air Force argued that the incident was a hoax, the investigation brought to light the type of evidence that is not easily faked and that may one day provide proof of a true "close encounter."

Dr. X

In 1968, a respected French physician who is known to the public only as Dr. X walked outdoors. He saw not the lightning that he had expected, but two identical disks hovering nearby. Each one was about 200 feet (61 meters) wide, 50 feet (15 meters) high, and topped by an antenna. Sparks shot between the two disks, Dr. X reported, and a streak of white light was beamed to the ground. He said that the disks merged into one and that he was hit by the beam of light at about the same time that he heard a loud noise and saw the disk disappear in a shower of sparks.

A couple of weeks after the encounter, the doctor noticed a small triangle of discolored skin around his navel. The patch disappeared and reappeared many times over a period of years.

TV Extraterrestrials and Modern Movie Aliens

The contemporary entertainment era has included a steady flow of science-fiction movies and television shows. In 1959, the movie *The Blob* gave us a look at an alien on the loose, oozing its way across America. Early science-fiction television shows featured the cartoon family the Jetsons, who zipped around space "sometime in the future." Comedian Robin Williams entertained us as Mork from the planet Ork, a lovable, confused, and zany alien on the show *Mork and Mindy*. Television shows such as *Lost in Space* and *Alf* intrigued us with adventurous as well as humorous looks at human/alien encounters. *Third*

There are many examples of friendly, sensitive aliens, such as the creature from the popular movie E.T. The Extra-Terrestrial.

Rock From the Sun depicted the many silly misunderstandings that might occur when aliens try to fit into earthling society.

In the 1970s and 1980s, we were treated to a variety of extraterrestrial tales on film that were enhanced by the very latest thinking on what aliens might look like and what they might want, as well as the most realistic of special effects. The trilogy of movies *Star Wars*, *Return of the Jedi*, and *The Empire Strikes Back* featured a hodgepodge of entertaining aliens, including the hairy, sensitive alien, Chewbacca, and the small, wooly creatures, the Ewoks. In 1982, viewers of all ages were charmed by the much-loved movie, *E.T. The Extra-Terrestrial*, the story of a stranded alien befriended by an earthling boy. *Close Encounters of the Third Kind* reflected our belief that aliens from outer space were coming, that we would eventually actually meet them, and that it would be a good experience.

Some films have focused on the darker side of alien/human interaction. Hideous creatures with violent intentions startled us in *The Thing* in 1982 and the *Alien* movies.

Sometime after the sighting, the doctor cut himself while chopping wood and the wound became infected. He also had an old wound that he had gotten during a mine explosion. Inexplicably, these wounds healed without treatment. Was this the result of a true close encounter?

Scientists Seek Proof

Scientists have their own list of what constitutes a real encounter with alien life. Logical evidence includes such indicators as burn marks on the ground, possibly caused by a spacecraft's engines, and indentations in the earth, presumably made by landing gear.

Other scientific evidence includes electrical forces that may affect people, animals, electrical equipment, and the ground. Rashes, burns, illness, and radioactivity are other side effects that would be considered evidence of encounters with aliens.

Scientists try to obtain evidence of alien encounters by collecting samples of burned grass, singed earth, or fragments of metal. Geiger counters are used to measure radiation levels, while magnetometers measure disturbances in the Earth's magnetic field.

Although computer-enhanced photographs would seem to be the best possible evidence of a UFO or an alien life-form, no such pictures yet exist. Photographs collected so far have either been declared fakes, are so unclear that scientists cannot draw conclusions from them, or are probably pictures of military aircraft.

Many sightings of UFOs have been reported, and some people claim they have actually been inside a spacecraft and have even met aliens. However, physical evidence of such events or beings is limited and has never proven any reported incident to be true.

People who claim to have encountered aliens often describe them as having large eyes and little or no nose.

What do scientists participating in SETI projects expect to find if they encounter a life-form from elsewhere in the universe?

To imagine what an alien life-form might look like, we would have to take into consideration the sciences of biology, ecology, climatology, anatomy, and zoology. All of these would affect how a life-form originated and evolved on a particular planet.

Many science-fiction writers and artists have used their creativity to speculate on the physical appearance of space beings. But probably no one has applied scientific thinking to his or her creative talent more than Wayne Douglas Barlowe, whose illustrations appear in *Barlowe's Guide to Extraterrestrials*. The incredible, amusing, often outrageous life-forms that Barlowe has created include humanoid, insectoid, reptilian, and other types of creatures. All of these are based on science-fiction writers' science-based ideas. So far, artistic and scientific guesses are just that—guesses.

The Roswell Incident

One of the most famous and well-documented cases of a reported, although never proven, visit by extraterrestrials to Earth began on the night of July 2, 1947. That night, there was a storm in the desert near Roswell, New Mexico. The next day, a local rancher found strange pieces of metal and wire, parchmentlike paper, and metal rods covered with writing that he could not decipher. He collected the material and turned it over to the local sheriff, who contacted federal authorities. The materials were described by one investigator as "nothing made on Earth."

At the same time, more than 100 miles (161 kilometers) away, another man discovered what looked like a crashed flying saucer. Beside it lay four small bodies with large heads, big, slanted eyes, and skinny arms and legs. The dead creatures were wearing tight one-piece gray suits.

Authorities carted off the disk and the bodies and warned witnesses not to discuss the incident. Later, the government said that the debris was the remains of a weather balloon.

To this day, there is no evidence in the public record indicating that anything extraordinary was recovered at this crash site. Although there were media reports of a government cover-up of a team of scientists known as the Majestic 12, who supposedly conducted autopsies on the alleged aliens, this has never been proved. An intriguing video showing blurred images of scientists examining odd-looking bodies has been broadcast on television, but it is unclear whether this video offers authentic proof of an "alien autopsy."

Hoaxes and Fakes

A percentage of UFO sightings have turned out to be deliberate hoaxes. The ways in which one could "fake" a sighting are limited only by the imagination.

In November 1952, a man named George Adamski returned from the California desert with a tale of meeting a handsome, long-haired alien from the planet Venus who communicated with him through sign language and mental telepathy. He insisted that the aliens would not let themselves be photographed. Adamski's photographs of Venusian "scout ships" turned out to be models made from chicken feeders and bottles.

In 1967, Dan and Grant Jaraslaw, two teenage brothers from Michigan, took pictures of a Frisbee™ in their backyard. For nine years, the photographs were accepted as evidence of a flying saucer appearing in daylight. Even after extensive examination of the photographs, experts could not prove that the photographs had been faked. It was only after the brothers confessed to their mischievous joke that the truth became known.

In another famous hoax in the 1960s, an engineer in Venezuela placed a photograph of a button at the top of

UFO hoaxes come in many forms. This "flying saucer" turned out to be made by a human being.

Some UFO mysteries remain unsolved. Here, a police officer in Bromley, England, examines a "flying saucer" found on a golf course in 1967.

an aerial shot of the Earth. He then photographed the combination, retouching the image to include not only the shadow of the "flying saucer" as it sped over the Earth, but also the shadow of the wing of the plane in which the photographer was supposedly flying. Like many particularly well-thought-out hoaxes, this one took a while for authorities to debunk.

Other hoaxes and fakes have included photos of airborne automobile hubcaps, optical illusions created in the taking or development of photographs, and the use of software to manipulate images with computers. The ability to produce convincing hoaxes increases as technology grows more sophisticated.

Extraterrestrials and Imagination

Of great interest to psychologists these days are the reasons why people claim that they have seen UFOs or have even been abducted by aliens. They are researching how behavior is shaped by social and cultural forces, which may include worries about personal security or environmental problems. Psychologists are also focusing on how people react and behave in stressful circumstances.

During the winter of 1989 and 1990, when the Berlin Wall—which had divided East and West Germany for years—was about to be dismantled, there was a rash of UFO sightings in the country of Belgium. Scientists wondered whether subconscious

The aurora borealis, or northern lights, can create otherworldly patterns in the night sky.

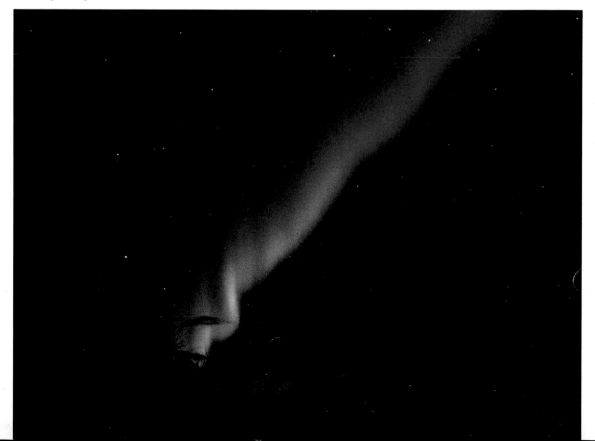

The Science of
Star Trek

One of the most intriguing things about science fiction is wondering how much is fiction and how much is science. Probably nowhere else is this fascinating combination more obvious than in the globally popular *Star Trek* series.

Star Trek was created by Gene Roddenberry and was first broadcast on television in 1966. Its captivating tales took place in the 24th century and involved such characters as Captain James T. Kirk, the pointed-eared Mr. Spock from the planet Vulcan, and the rest of the crew of the *Starship Enterprise*. Their mission was "to boldly go where no man has gone before." Viewers of the show were captivated by the "futuristic" technology used by the crew to travel to different worlds, and were enthralled by the unique alien life that the *Enterprise* crew encountered.

Star Trek had thousands of loyal followers when it went off the air in 1969. It quickly reappeared in new forms: as an animated cartoon television series; as full-length motion pictures; and as three new television shows based on, and taking place 70 years after, the original series.

While some of the inventive aspects of the various shows are clearly the imaginings of writers, artists, and special effects wizards, much of *Star Trek* is based on real science and emerging technologies. (A goal of Gene Roddenberry's was to have a scientific explanation for the different things that the series presented.)

The galaxies that starships visit in *Star Trek* are reachable because the ships can travel at incredible speeds, using powerful fuels. The distances covered by such ships as the *Enterprise* might be possible if black holes could be used as short cuts through the universe. Also, the possibility exists that antimatter (a fuel for *Star Trek* ships) may propel rockets one day.

Michael Westmore, a creator of *Star Trek*'s alien life-forms, admits that he examines such magazines as *National Geographic* and *Ranger Rick* for ideas. The current look of the show's Klingons, for example, was inspired by a picture of a cross section of dinosaur vertebrae.

One aspect of the series—the holodeck—seems possible in the future when it is compared to virtual reality headgear, gloves, and boots that some people use today to have fun. In the new *Star Trek* shows, crew members can spend time in the holodeck—a place where characters interact with three-dimensional, computer-generated images.

The robotics seen on *Star Trek* are fantasy turning to fact. Space and underwater robotic probes are now used on, above, and beneath Earth's surface. Scientists are also currently working on human-looking robots with electric-motor muscles, steel bones, and plastic skin. In *Star Trek*, a character called Data is an android who is a high-ranking member of the crew.

Star Trek's producers do pull our legs now and then by making the familiar—saltshakers and potato peelers, just to name two household items—look like futuristic space gadgetry.

Curiously, science fiction sometimes has trouble keeping up with science fact. When the original *Star Trek* series first appeared there were no such things as personal computers, hand-held calculators, or tiny portable phones similar to the communicator used by Captain Kirk. Producers of the current shows admit that some of the technology they try to project into the *Star Treks* of the future will probably be surpassed on Earth in a mere 10 to 20 years.

Leonard Nimoy's character, the Vulcan Mr. Spock (seen here on the lower right), is probably the best-known alien on television.

fears regarding the re-unification of a country that had invaded Belgium twice had inspired a sudden flurry of "sightings."

Psychologists also considered whether people who witnessed such phenomena as earthquake lights, the aurora borealis, and will-o'-the-wisps (swamp or marsh gas) could be psychologically unstable enough to interpret fairly common natural occurrences as UFO sightings.

One French ufologist, Michel Monnerie, believes that psychologists and sociologists, not physicists and aviation experts, should conduct UFO studies. He contends that people today are "sighting" many of the same objects or phenomena that people of ancient times did. Ancient peoples had only their gods to explain such mysteries. Today, however, interpretations of unexplained sightings are based on a much more highly developed system of scientific knowledge.

What Have They Seen?

Many of the people who claim to have seen UFOs are ordinary citizens who seem to truly believe that what they have seen is real. Usually, however, these witnesses have misinterpreted something as unremarkable as a reflection on a window or have misidentified something as common as an aircraft seen from an odd angle or under unusual lighting conditions. It is also difficult for untrained observers to report accurately the size, distance, or speed of an object in the sky. This is especially true if they have seen it only briefly, in poor light, or at night.

Some witnesses may be influenced by subconscious forces that they are not even aware of. Some psychologists believe that certain people "need" to see UFOs and so they do. Some people give their sightings some religious significance, transforming their own hopes and fears into a fantasy.

Space Brothers and Sisters

The first people to say that they had actually had contact with alien beings were members of religious cults in California in the 1940s. Most lived near military test sites in the Arizona, New Mexico, or Nevada deserts—locations of early UFO reports.

These "contactees," as they were called, insisted that they had not only seen flying saucers but had also met their crews. The aliens, they proclaimed, were very humanlike, often beautiful, and eager to talk to humans and to explain what they were doing on Earth. It appeared that the aliens were monitoring nuclear tests and attempts by earthlings to travel through space. They were here to warn us, reported the contactees, that we were upsetting the balance of the universe.

These friendly extraterrestrials were referred to as "space brothers and sisters" and were believed to act as guides and tutors. Contactees reported that they would often meet with the space beings, be invited to tour the spacecraft, and perhaps even be taken on a trip to the aliens' home planet.

Members of such "UFO cults" were eager to share their stories through books, articles, and appearances on radio and television. But improved research and technology disproved many of the cults' claims. High-powered telescopes and space probes proved that beings from space could not have come from the moon or Mars and other nearby planets, as the cultists had claimed.

Alien Diversity

A short, glowing alien with bulging yellow eyes. A long-armed, no-necked, wrinkled, gray alien. Scaly beings dressed in white body suits! Does this sound like the stuff of comic books? Well, many of us do get our first ideas of what alien life-forms might look like from the comics, and we have done so for more than 60 years.

Early comic-strip adventurers such as Buck Rogers traveled by spaceship to other planets, where they encountered evil extraterrestrials. Flash Gordon zipped around space in an atom-propelled spaceship.

The aliens that these characters encountered ranged from ugly and mean to mild-mannered, near-earthlings. Astronomer Carl Sagan has one thing to say about the extraterrestrials that have been created in fiction or that have supposedly been seen by earthlings: boring! He believes that beings that more or less resemble earthlings—no matter how elongated, bug-eyed, or otherworldly looking—are not very imaginative when compared with what natural forces could concoct.

If we examine the array of life-forms that have evolved on Earth, ranging from the dinosaur to the jellyfish, we can begin to imagine what Sagan has in mind. Depending on the biological and ecological conditions of a planet, almost any type of life-form is possible. In fact, one that we can actually imagine is probably the least likely of all!

Are You an Alien?

Science-fiction movies such as *Starman* and *The Man Who Fell to Earth* express the interest and belief in the intriguing possibility that not only are "aliens among us" but also "aliens are us." Some present-day cult members insist that there are many descendants of alien visitors living, working, and going to school among earthlings.

Supposedly, their ancestors were beings who came to our planet from elsewhere in the universe. These cultists say that extra vertebrae, unusual blood types, low body temperature, and chronic sinusitis are proof of alien ancestry. Cultists believe these so-called Star People are here to help earthlings prepare for possible future upheavals, such as major geological changes and the collapse of social organizations.

Channeling

There are people who are very involved in channeling, which is when spirit guides supposedly speak their messages through humans. Some cultists believe that channeling is done through alien guides.

Two groups that believe in alien ancestry and channeling of messages from space through humans have been around for many years. The Aetherius Society was founded in London, England, in 1954 by George King, a taxi driver. He claimed that he was contacted by an extraterrestrial "intelligence" that informed King that he would serve as its voice on Earth. The Unarius Academy of Science, based in San Diego, California, holds an annual convention at which a channel, Uriel, claims to receive messages of peace and love from other planets.

Most people think that members of such cults imagine these messages. Until cult members can provide proof of the origin of the messages that they say they receive, they have little to offer to serious searches for extraterrestrial life.

This "UFO photo" was taken February 7, 1966, by a man named Ralph Ditter, one of thousands of people who say they have had a close encounter.

CHAPTER 4

3, 2, 1: CONTACT!

Imagine being the astronomer who gets e-mail saying that we have just intercepted a message from an alien life-form. This, say scientists, is the most likely way we initially would be notified that an Earth-based radio telescope had received such a signal from space. With the discovery of information of new planets and the aid of ever more sophisticated space telescopes and probes, the answer to the question "Are we alone?" may be just around the galactic corner.

Life on Mars?

One planet scientists believe may sustain extraterrestrial life is Mars. Much of what we know about the Martian climate comes from the two *Viking* missions of the mid-1970s. More recently, the Hubble space telescope has shown that the information scientists have about the planet's climate may represent only one phase of a long, complex weather cycle. The Hubble telescope has found clouds over Mars, which indicates that water is freezing out of the planet's atmosphere. Other information seems to confirm that Mars has, not only the "hot" summer season that scientists are familiar with, but a cold season as well. Although either season is too extreme for human beings, we cannot be sure that the same is true for another life-form.

Some people have been especially interested in a geological formation revealed in photos returned to Earth from a *Mariner* probe in 1976. This formation, known as the Face of Mars, resembles a human face looking out into space. Nearby is a group of pyramid-shaped structures, which some people think has the appearance of a city. There are those who think that the face and the pyramids look as if they were created by intelligent beings. Most scientists, though, are confident that they occurred as a result of natural forces.

New Planets Offer New Opportunities

Many people object to the idea of extraterrestrial life. They say that Earth is unique and that only wishful thinking and a healthy imagination make others believe in such illogical

War of the Worlds!

It can be both amusing and frightening to speculate on how humans would react to an actual visit from an extraterrestrial. One true historic incident may have given an indication of how ordinary citizens would react if aliens in spaceships ever landed on Earth.

On October 30, 1938, Orson Welles's Mercury Theatre broadcast a realistic dramatization of the book *The War of the Worlds*, by H. G. Wells, on CBS radio. The fictional story tells of the invasion of Earth by Martians. The broadcast was preceded by an announcement explaining what would follow. Many people, however, either did not pay attention to the statement or tuned in after the tale had already begun.

As the dramatic story progressed, many listeners believed that they were hearing a live news report and panicked. Because the story was set in Trenton, New Jersey, people up and down the Eastern seaboard fled into the streets in terror. Some people took out their guns and prepared to protect their families from the alien invasion.

Orson Welles apologized the next day for the misunderstanding, but the damage was done. We saw for ourselves how we might respond to extraterrestrials landing on Earth. Is it any wonder that *if* they are here, they keep it a secret?!

Amazingly, many people who heard Orson Welles's The War of the Worlds *radio broadcast actually believed that aliens had landed on Earth.*

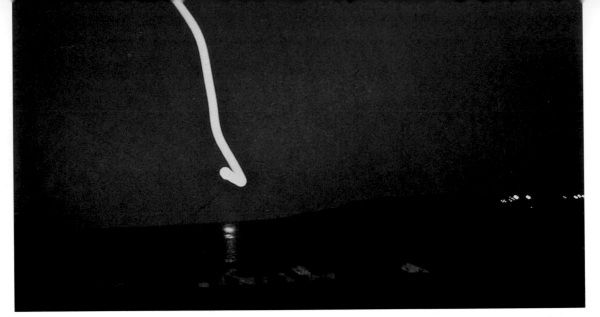

UFO sightings such as this one may be frauds, but there are scientists who believe we cannot rule out the possibility of life elsewhere in the universe.

things as UFOs and aliens. But when these same people are confronted with statistics about the universe, some change their minds about the possibility of life existing elsewhere.

Most cosmologists—people who study space—believe that the universe was born about 15 billion years ago in an enormous explosion of energy called the Big Bang. Since then, the universe has been expanding and cooling. Between 5 billion and 10 billion years ago, large clouds of gas drawn together by gravity began to unite. Stars began to form in these clouds and to create the millions of galaxies that exist today.

During the Big Bang, hydrogen and helium were produced. Heavier elements, such as carbon, oxygen, nitrogen, sulfur, and phosphorus were "cooked up" later in the centers of massive stars. These chemical elements are the ones that make up most of our planet and our bodies. And these are the building blocks that scientists believe are essential for the formation of life. Scientists believe that the most likely place to find such building blocks, other than on Earth, is on other planets.

For a long time, scientists have been seeking to prove the existence of other planets outside our solar system. They believe that this discovery would increase the chance of finding extraterrestrial life. Scientists have varying theories about what we may discover outside our solar system. For example, most astronomers believe that there are planets out among the stars still undiscovered. In fact, in 1995 and 1996, different groups of scientists in Switzerland and the United States found what they believe is evidence of previously unknown planets orbiting stars similar to our Sun. Could there, then, be other forms of life in our galaxy? There are scientists who argue that, if there are so many planets, it is likely that some of them have life-conducive conditions. At least one of these celestial bodies appears to be the right temperature for water to exist—which means that life might be able to exist there!

The Search Heats Up

The recent discovery of two planets has intensified the search for life beyond Earth. Scientists are expanding their survey of distant celestial bodies in hopes of finding additional planets. In December 1996, NASA will launch the *Mars Pathfinder*. When this spacecraft lands on Mars in 1997, it will look for fossil remains of microbes or other simple life-forms.

NASA is also planning a multitelescope spacecraft that will photograph Earthlike planets for signs of life. The launch of this new vehicle is scheduled for 2010. This "planet finder"

Goldstone Deep Space Network in California is one of the places conducting an all-sky search for extraterrestrial life.

will orbit the Sun out as far as Jupiter and will be 40 times more powerful than the Hubble space telescope. A smaller version of this spacecraft could be launched as early as 2003 and will orbit Earth on a test mission.

Scientists have little hope of finding life on the two newly discovered planets, because they appear to lack the critical and most basic life-sustaining elements like oxygen and organic chemicals. However, one of the planets does have an estimated temperature of 185°F (85°C). That is cool enough for water to exist in liquid form, so there may be the possibility of some type of life there.

A number of scientific searches for extraterrestrial life, discussed in Chapter 2, are ongoing. The Billion Channel Extraterrestrial Assay, or BETA, which began in October 1995, continues its search using a billion channels on the observatory's highly powerful telescope.

During the summer of 1995, Project Phoenix at the SETI Institute in Mountain View, California, scanned 200 stars within

155 light-years of Earth. It is expanding its survey to include 800 nearby stars that are similar to the Sun. This search will continue until the end of the decade.

Alien Abductions

Although it would be exciting to catch a glimpse of a UFO zooming through the heavens (and, perhaps, to see the extraterrestrials inside), it would be another matter indeed to be abducted, or kidnapped, by aliens.

In the United States, millions of people claim to have seen a UFO. And thousands say that they have actually seen, been contacted by, or been abducted by alien beings!

Some of these people report that they were given medical examinations by aliens or had tiny metal implants put into their bodies. These implants supposedly are used by aliens to monitor the whereabouts of abductees after they are returned to Earth. Some people claim that the implants give them extraordinary psychic powers.

Many of the abduction stories have amazing similarities, such as periods of missing time. Yet, except for haunting memories, an odd scar, or the removal of implants of an undetermined origin, not one person has been able to provide definite proof of such an extraordinary event as alien abduction.

One of the most famous alien abduction stories is that of Betty and Barney Hill. Their adventure began on September 19, 1961. The case is one of the earliest such events ever reported. The Hills were driving through the White Mountains of New Hampshire when they realized that a light in the sky seemed

The Mystery of
Crop Circles

There are many unexplained phenomena on Earth for which, some people believe, extraterrestrials are responsible. One example is crop circles—the curious rings of flattened crops that have mysteriously appeared in fields around the world for hundreds of years, since medieval times.

In the crop circles, the stalks of the crops have been tightly compressed, as if a great weight had been put on them. The stalks may form a swirl. Crop circles range from a small 18 inches (46 centimeters) to more than 200 feet (61 meters) across. Although they have been found around the world, especially in the United States, Australia, France, and Japan, they are most common in the English counties of Wiltshire and Hampshire.

Are crop circles the landing sites of alien spacecraft? In 1966, an Australian man was driving by a farm when he noticed what looked like a spaceship rising out of a swamp. Upon exploring the site, he found a circular depression 30 feet (9 meters) wide with three smaller, deeper indentations inside the circle. The reeds were flattened into a circular pattern.

There could be a logical explanation for the crop circles. Farm machinery

to be following their car. When they stopped to look at the light with binoculars, they saw a curved shape, seemingly dotted with windows. At the windows, Barney Hill saw figures wearing what appeared to be uniforms.

At first, the Hills assumed that the vehicle was a military helicopter. But the longer they watched the brilliantly lit vehicle, the closer it moved toward them. Barney Hill felt that he was about to be captured by these beings, whatever they were. He jumped back into his car, and he and his wife sped home.

could make them—but probably not in the middle of the night and certainly not in medieval times. Even downdrafts from helicopters could not produce the swirling pattern beneath low power lines, where crop circles sometimes appear.

Some physicists wonder whether electric power affecting the Earth's magnetic field had caused the crop circles, but the magnitude of power required would be too great. A combination of electrostatically charged dust and pollen gathered into a glowing whirlwind is one meteorologist's theory. In fact, everything from chemicals, lightning, toadstool fungi, and rampaging hedgehogs have been accused of creating these strange circles. A few have been easily identified as hoaxes.

This crop formation appeared near Hungerford, England, mystifying local residents.

While people in the past blamed the devil for these circles, some ufologists today think that the circles are UFO landing sites and that their shapes may even represent a message from outer space.

But that was not the end of their story. Betty began having nightmares of being taken with Barney aboard a spacecraft and being examined by aliens. Her husband began to experience so much anxiety that he sought the help of a psychiatrist. When he tried to relate the events of that evening, he realized that he could not account for two hours of time. Since the Hills reported this event, many others who believe they have experienced alien abduction believe that time has passed for which they cannot account.

Under hypnosis, conducted separately, the Hills told identical tales. Both said that they had met humanoid creatures with large, wraparound eyes, no noses, and slitlike mouths. They recalled being aboard a spaceship and receiving medical examinations. Betty reproduced a map of a star system that, she said, the aliens had shown her.

No proof was ever found of the Hills's abduction, which was widely reported by the media and was later the subject of a 1966 book by John Fuller, *The Interrupted Journey*, and a 1975 NBC television movie, "The UFO Incident."

The Walton Incident

Travis Walton alleged that he was abducted by aliens on November 5, 1975. Supposedly, this abduction was witnessed by six people. Walton said that he was walking in a forest in Arizona when he was suddenly knocked unconscious by a beam of light that came from a UFO hovering overhead. Walton was then taken aboard the craft.

Once aboard, Walton says, he saw three short humanoid creatures that were wearing coveralls. They placed Walton on a table and put something like an oxygen mask on his face. The next thing that Walton remembered was awakening on the ground near Heber, Arizona. As he lay there, he reports, a circular UFO arose from a highway and disappeared into the sky. Five days had passed between Walton's disappearance and his return to Earth.

Walton's tale of alien abduction is similar to many other such reports, especially the parts about meeting humanoid creatures, being placed on a table, and the experience of missing time. Although it was reported that Walton failed a lie-detector test when questioned about the events, the public's imagination was stirred by such a vivid encounter, supposedly witnessed by others. In 1993, a movie, *Fire in the Sky*, was made about Walton's alleged abduction. It was another in a long line of such stories, entertaining but unsubstantiated by any type of hard and reliable proof.

Are people who claim to have been abducted by extraterrestrials crazy? Some mental-health professionals believe that such individuals simply have wild imaginations or emotional problems. But other psychiatrists, psychologists, and therapists who have worked with abductees think this is a fascinating phenomenon that deserves more serious attention.

How Close Are We to Discovering Extraterrestrial Life?

Scientists are enthusiastic about the possibility of discovering extraterrestrial life. Between the discovery of new planets and the ever-improving tools available for searches, some even believe that such a discovery is not far off. And some scientists suspect that the universe is teeming with life. If a microbe or a simple single-cell organism was actually discovered on another planet, it would certainly fuel our imaginations and speed the search for additional, perhaps more advanced life-forms.

Human beings have always had so many questions about the possibility of life elsewhere in space. Perhaps the answer to the question "Are we alone?" will come in our lifetime!

abduct To carry off by force; to kidnap.

alien A being from someplace other than Earth.

all-sky survey A non-targeted radio signal search of space.

android A computerized creature made to resemble a human.

antimatter The opposite of matter; made of antiparticles; not yet observed by scientists.

astronomy The study of celestial bodies.

aurora borealis Luminous bands of light in the night skies of the far north caused by charged particles in the Earth's magnetic field. Also called northern lights.

ball lightning Unusual form of lightning that is ball-shaped.

Big Bang The explosion of matter that marked the beginning of time and the creation of the universe.

black hole A place in space with such a strong gravitational force that not even light can escape from it.

channel A person who supposedly receives messages in his or her mind from aliens to be transmitted to others.

constellation A formation of stars that creates a pattern.

cosmologist One who studies space.

cult The enthusiastic devotion of a group to a particular person, thing, or idea.

exobiology The search for and study of extraterrestrial life.

extraterrestrial Anything that exists outside of Earth and its atmosphere.

galaxy A large group of stars and their associated gas and dust.

gravity The force of attraction between two celestial bodies.

hoax An intentional trick or fake.

humanoid A being with human form.

interstellar Between the stars.

light-year The distance that light travels in a vacuum in one year, or 5.9 trillion miles (9.5 trillion kilometers).

meteorite A mass of stone or metal that falls to Earth from outer space.

mirage An image created by an optical illusion that appears to be real, but is not.

optical illusion A deceptive visual image.

oscilloscope An electronic instrument that measures voltage and current.

parallel world Theoretically, a place existing at the same place and time as the world we know.

phenomenon; phenomena (pl.) Any fact or occurrence; often refers to an unusual happening.

pictograph Picture symbol.

planet A celestial body that orbits a star.

radio telescope An instrument used to

detect and record radio waves coming from objects in space.

radio wave An electromagnetic wave within the range of radio frequencies.

robotics The science and technology of robot design.

skeptic One who doubts that something exists or is true.

solar system The Sun and the planets and other bodies that orbit it.

spores The reproductive parts of ferns and mosses.

telepathic Having the ability to communicate with the mind.

ufologist One who studies unidentified flying objects.

universe All the things that exist in space.

virtual reality An artificial environment that appears realistic, but is created with computers and software programs.

will-o'-the-wisp A glowing light that moves over a marsh; it is caused by a gas that can catch fire.

FURTHER READING

Angelo, Joseph A., Jr. *The Extraterrestrial Encyclopedia.* New York: Facts On File, 1991.

Asimov, Isaac. *Unidentified Flying Objects.* Milwaukee, WI: Gareth Stevens Publishing, 1989.

Darling, David J. *The New Astronomy: An Ever-Changing Universe.* Minneapolis, MN: Dillon Press, 1985.

Krauss, Lawrence M. *The Physics of Star Trek.* Basic Books, 1995.

Landau, Elaine. *UFOs.* Brookfield, CT: Millbrook Press, 1995.

Makower, Joel, ed. *The Air & Space Catalog: The Complete Sourcebook to Everything in the Universe.* New York: Vintage Books, 1989.

Marsh, Carole. *How to Find an Extraterrestrial in Your Own Backyard.* Atlanta: Gallopade Publishing Group, 1992.

Ritchie, David. *UFO: The Definitive Guide to Unidentified Flying Objects and Related Phenomena.* New York: Facts On File, 1994.

Williams, Richard, Senior Editor. *UFO: The Continuing Enigma.* New York: Reader's Digest, 1991.

WHERE TO CALL IF YOU SEE A UFO

UFO Reporting Center, a 24-hour UFO reporting line (206) 772-3000

WHERE TO WRITE FOR MORE INFORMATION

Ames Research Center
SETI Office, Code SI
Moffett Field, CA 94035-1000

Center for UFO Studies
1609 Sherman Avenue
Evanston, IL 60201

J. Allen Hynek Center
  for UFO Studies (CUFOS)
2457 West Peterson
Chicago, IL 60659

Jet Propulsion Laboratory
California Institute of Technology
SETI Office, 303-401
4800 Oak Grove Drive
Pasadena, CA 91109-8099

Mutual UFO Network (MUFON)
103 Oldtowne Road
Seguin, TX 78155

National Space Society (NSS)
922 Pennsylvania Avenue, SE
Washington, DC 20003

Planetary Society
65 North Catalina Avenue
Pasadena, CA 91106

SETI Institute
2035 Landings Drive
Mountain View, CA 94043

ON-LINE

SETI Institute (http://www.seti-inst.edu)

UFO Norway (http://www.norconnect.no/~brenne/ufonor_e.htm)
National UFO investigation organization with a web site that features articles, photos, and news updates.

British UFO Research Association, BUFORA On-Line
(http://www.citadel.co.uk/citadel/eclipse/futura/bufora/bufora.htm)
Home page for the largest UFO research organization in the UK.

Extraterrestrial Biological Entity (EBE) Page (http://www.ee.fit.edu/users/lpinto/)
Information on ETs, abduction stories, photos, movies, and a discussion and testimonial forum.

The Internet UFO Group (http://users.aol.com/IUFOG/)

Alien Information (http://www.iinet.com.au/~ bertino/alien.htm)

SOURCES

Angelo, Joseph A., Jr. *The Extraterrestrial Encyclopedia.* New York: Facts On File, 1991.

Asimov, Isaac. *Unidentified Flying Objects.* Milwaukee, WI: Gareth Stevens Publishing, 1989.

Barlowe, Wayne Douglas, Summers, Ian, and Meacham, Beth. *Barlowe's Guide to Extraterrestrials.* New York: Workman Publishing, 1979.

Brokaw, Tom. NBC Nightly News. "Billion Channel Extraterrestrial Array." October 30, 1995.

"CUFOS." J. Allen Hynek Center for UFO Studies, Chicago, IL, pp. 1–6.

Darling, David J. *The New Astronomy: An Ever-Changing Universe.* Minneapolis, MN: Dillon Press, 1985.

Goodman, Billy. *Air & Space.* "Ancient Whispers." April/May, 1992, pp. 55–61.

Krauss, Lawrence M. *The Physics of Star Trek.* Basic Books, 1995.

Lane, Earl. "Super Rays from Outer Space." Washington, D.C.: *Newsday*, November 5, 1995.

Lightman, Alan. *Time for the Stars.* New York: Viking, 1992.

Makower, Joel, ed. *The Air & Space Catalog: The Complete Sourcebook to Everything in the Universe.* New York: Vintage Books, 1989.

"NASA Microwave Observing Project." SETI Office, Ames Research Center, Moffet Field, CA. June, 1990, pp. 1–32.

Olson, Tim. "The Science of Star Trek." The New Explorers video series. Chicago and Kurtis Productions, Ltd., 1995.

Ritchie, David. *UFO: The Definitive Guide to Unidentified Flying Objects and Related Phenomena.* New York: Facts On File, 1994.

"SETI." NASA, Jet Propulsion Laboratory, California Institute of Technology, Pasadena, CA. January, 1990, pp. 1–10.

Sobel, Dava. *Life.* "The Search for a Real E.T." September, 1992, pp. 61–67.

"Some Frequently Asked SETI Questions & Answers." SETI Institute.

White, Frank. *The SETI Factor.* New York: Walker and Company, 1990.

Wilford, John Noble. *Mars Beckons.* New York: Knopf, 1990.

INDEX